The 5 Critical Attributes Needed to Win the FAITH Fight

The 5 Critical Attributes Needed to Win the FAITH Fight

PAUL L. DENMAN, PH.D.

Hunter Entertainment Network
Colorado Springs, Colorado

The 5 Critical Attributes Needed to Win the Faith Fight
Copyright © 2018 by Paul L. Denman, Ph.D.
First Edition: May 2018

No part of this book may be reproduced or transmitted in any form or by any means without written permission of the publisher, except in brief quotes or reviews.

To order products, or for any other correspondence:

Hunter Entertainment Network
4164 Austin Bluffs Parkway, Suite 214
Colorado Springs, Colorado 80918
www.hunter-ent-net.com
Tel. (253) 906-2160 – Fax: (719) 528-6359
E-mail: contact@hunter-entertainment.com
Or reach us on Facebook at: Hunter Entertainment Network
"Offering God's Heart to a Dying World"

This book and all other Hunter Entertainment Network™ Hunter Heart Publishing™, and Hunter Heart Kids™ books are available at Christian bookstores and distributors worldwide.

Chief Editor: Gord Dormer
Book cover design: Phil Coles Independent Design
Layout & logos: Exousia Marketing Group
www.exousiamg.com

ISBN: 978-1-937741-26-6

Printed in the United States of America.

Dedication

To the King eternal, immortal, invisible, the only God, be honor and glory forever and ever. Amen. This work is dedicated to the source from which it came: my Lord and Savior, Jesus Christ – the author and finisher of my faith.

To my wife of over forty-five years without whose winds of faith and love I would not be able fly at such heights.

To my children and grandchildren who always surround me with love immeasurable.

To my pastor and associates for their devotion to unwaveringly teach the truth of God's Word with clarity and understanding.

To my church family who surrounds me with their prayers and love unending.

To the Body of Christ all over this planet who "fight the good fight of faith" every day. May the words contained within focus your faith, remind you of your true self, and give you Hope!

Finally, to my fellow laborers in the work of biblical therapeutics, (the healing of souls by changing their beliefs) the Therapon Practitioners.

Foreword

Finally, a book with Godly wisdom and instruction for not only walking in faith, but *becoming* faith! Dr. Paul Denman has had a desire for the creation of this book for over twenty years. However, it was not until he actually applied these principles in his own walk, as a man of God, that he knew what was needed. For approximately 40+ years these concepts became the reality of "walking out" his own salvation.

This manuscript has come through prayer and the practical application of God's truth in his personal trials. One thing he has grown to understand is the lack of faith will not produce success, but, when we trust God and apply faith, we grow, and the will of God brings the success of the transformation into who we are meant to be. As we often hear Dr. Denman say, it is a daily choice to trust God and step out in faith. Our challenge is to believe and apply these principles or not. One of Dr. Denman's greatest attributes is his willingness to stay humble before God and man. The opportunity for success is freely available. However, the decision is every person's personal choice. This book is a result of his decision to remain accountable and teachable. The evidence is in his teachings.

As I read and studied what was expressed in his teachings, I found great joy in the examples and practicality of our need for the greater measure of our relationship with our Lord and Savior Jesus Christ. Faith comes by hearing and hearing by the Word of God. In this passage, the word, 'Word', is defined as the revelation, or understanding, of God's written, or logos, Word.

Dr. Denman has done an exceptional job making certain that all who read this manuscript is well-equipped with the need for the understanding and the application of faith in our lives as Believers. I encourage you to acquire this book for all new Believers, as well as those struggling to remain strong in their daily walk. The seeds of truth in this writing will never return void, but will accomplish all God intended for anyone who reads, studies, and applies it.

Pastor Carolyn Bounds
Consuming Hearts Ministries
Houston, Texas

Table of Contents

Introduction 1

Attribute 1: Know That God Truly Exists and Act Like It! 7

Attribute 2: Believe In Your Covenant Right as God's Child 25

Attribute 3: Take Corresponding Action or Kinetic Faith 33

Attribute 4: Develop Your Faith… Spend Time With God .. 47

Attribute 5: Be Entirely Persuaded! 57

Conclusion: Covenant of Faith 85

About the Author 91

Bibliography 93

Introduction

"Then God said, 'Let us make man in our own image, after our likeness: and let them have dominion... male and female created he them.'"

In his book *Understanding Your Potential*, Myles Monroe [i] very clearly explains that God spoke to the source of everything that He created. The key here is to understand that when God created you, He spoke to Himself and out of Him came you. An indestructible, divinely spiritual entity made in the image of its Creator; with all rights, privileges, and capabilities hereunto appertaining thereof. The pursuit of understanding and applying not just a theoretical, but applicable lifestyle of faith requires accepting as a part of your belief system, two fundamental constructs: (1) God is real and we must live like it and (2) God is motivated by faith. I truly believe that most Christians, even those who profess to be in the "household of faith," know about God, but don't truly know Him.

After receiving the instructions directly from Christ, the disciples went about spreading the Word through the teachings of Christ and telling others of the great miracles and lessons that He taught. During this time, the disciples and their new recruits were known simply as *believers*. This was a very accurate name because as it is written in the Word "those who come to God must come in faith believing that He is the rewarder of them that diligently seek him." Actually, the Bible from beginning to end is the story about believing; about how God achieved building a world through the efforts of people who dared to believe Him.

For some reason, it totally escapes me that we live in a world today where even those people who call themselves Christians work very hard to complicate a rather simple truth: God is! People tried to create new gods or tried to shape the one God into a god that fits the truth they acquiesce to instead of what God has established as truth. The Bible is divided into two sections: The Old Testament and the New Testament. The Old Testament is referred to as the Gospel <u>concealed</u> in the New Testament, the Gospel <u>revealed</u>. The Bible clearly states that the Word of God (the Bible) is truth. In the book of Ecclesiastes, as I paraphrase, "God made man and His Word very plain, very simple, but in all of man's worldliness or attempts to create our *own truth*, we have found many ways to complicate truth."

This writing is an attempt to clarify and simplify why next to salvation, the most important lesson to be learned by Christians/Believers is *faith*. It is my sincere hope that by walking in faith, you will find life more rewarding, more peaceful, and more purposeful. Praise God!

Attribute #1

Know That God Truly Exists and Act Like It!

Attribute Number One:

Know That God Truly Exists and Act Like It!

"But without faith it is impossible to please him: for he that comes to God must believe that He is and that He is a rewarder of them that diligently seek Him."
(Hebrews 11:6)

"Now faith is confidence in what we hope for and assurance about what <u>we do not see</u>." (Hebrews 11:1)

If your sense-realm can evidence it, faith is not needed. That is, if you can make what is desired via taste, touch, hear, smell, or sight, you don't need faith.

- ❖ <u>By faith</u> we understand that the universe was formed at God's command.

- ❖ <u>By faith</u> Abel brought God a better offering than Cain did.
- ❖ <u>By faith</u> Enoch was taken from this life … he was commended as one who pleased God.
- ❖ <u>By faith</u> Noah, when warned about things not yet seen, in holy fear, built an ark to save his family.
- ❖ <u>By faith</u> Abraham, when called to go to a place he would later receive as his inheritance, made his home in the Promised Land.
- ❖ And <u>by faith</u> even Sarah, who was past childbearing age, was enabled to bear children because she considered Him faithful who had made the promise.

In this verse of scripture, God through the writings of the apostle Paul clearly gives us examples of how Noah (for example) pleased God by living the lifestyle of faith. Not a drop of rain fell upon the Earth when God instructed him to build an Ark. He had a word from God and responded by following His instruction to the letter.

The word 'faith' is used in many ways by many different cultures and religious sects. Most often, it is used to define someone's religious denomination. Speaking totally from a biblical perspective, faith is an action word. For example, Jesus told the woman with the issue blood *"your faith has made you whole."* In other words, something she did (in faith) caused her to be healed. Let me give a more humanistic example. A woman (I use a woman for this example because her emotional feelings and relationship to those feelings are more apropos to the example I'm trying to give) may be told by a man with whom she's romantically involved that he loves her. Usually, the first time he says that, she will not believe. Therefore, she does not act like she believes. She goes on in the relationship with the hopes that somehow, over a period of time, something will be done to cause her to believe that what he says is true and only then she can make a decision to return the feeling. In most cases, if he says it over and over again, eventually she will begin to believe that what he says is true (repetitious information with corresponding action). After which, she can then make a decision to act upon that which she now believes and look forward to the extension of that relationship.

So, too, is our faith. Another very good example is found in the first chapter of the Gospel according to Luke where Mary receives an angel with the message from God. The operative verse will be number 38. There Mary says, *"Behold, I am the handmaid of the Lord; be it unto me according to what you have said."* She made a decision to believe what she had heard.

Therefore, even though she had not had any sexual contact with a man, God would make her the mother of His only Son. Her faith and willingness to act on it pleased God because her 'action' faith made possible the entrance on the planet God's only Son who would win for Him a holy people, returning dominance of the earth to mankind. Recall that Adam had given up that right to Satan by his lack of faith and disobedience.

This story was taken from an article in *Looking Forward Magazine*[ii]:

A miracle is not the suspension of natural law, but the operation of a higher law. A man was sleeping at night in his cabin when suddenly, his room filled with light and the Savior appeared. The Lord told the man that He had work for him to do, and showed him a large rock in front of his cabin. The Lord explained that the man was to push against the rock with all his might. Why? What was the purpose? Understanding faith requires that we accept the fact that God gives us information on a "need to know basis" AND He determines what you need to know and when! The man did as instructed, day after day. For many years, he toiled from sun up to sun down, his shoulders set squarely against the cold, massive surface of the unmoving rock, pushing with all his might.

The 5 Critical Attributes Needed to Win the Faith Fight

Each night the man returned to his cabin sore, and worn out, feeling that his whole day had been spent in vain. Seeing that the man was showing signs of discouragement, the Adversary decided to enter the picture by placing thoughts into the man's weary mind: "You have been pushing against that rock for a long time, and it hasn't budged. Why kill yourself over this? You are never going to move it." The man began to anguish and fall into deep depression, because he considered not moving the rock made him a failure. These thoughts discouraged and disheartened the man.

"Why kill myself over this?" he thought. "I'll just put in my time, giving just the minimum effort, and that will be good enough." And that is what he planned to do until one day, he decided to make it a matter of prayer and take his troubled thoughts to the Lord. "Lord," he said, "I have labored long and hard in Your service, putting all my strength to do that which You have asked. Yet, after all this time, I have not even budged that rock by half a millimeter. What is wrong? Why am I failing?"

The Lord responded compassionately, "My child, when I asked you to serve Me and you accepted, I told you that your task was to push against the rock with all your strength, which you have done. Never once did I mention to you that I expected you to move it. Your task was to push. And now you come to me, with your strength spent, thinking that you have failed. But, is that really so? Look at yourself. Your arms (faith) are strong and muscled, your back (belief) sinew and brown, your hands are callused from constant pressure (prayer), and your legs (resolve) have become massive and hard. Through opposition, you have grown much and your abilities now surpass that which you used to have. Yet, you haven't moved the rock. But your calling was to be obedient and to push and to exercise your faith and trust in My wisdom. This you have done. I, My child, will now move the rock.

One of the most fundamental skills of operating in faith is that of obedience. Logically, faith is not logical. But faith begins when the will of God is known. It is neither subject to societal trends nor the logic of mankind.

I was a young college student when man first landed on the moon. I often marveled at how NASA could receive a signal from a relatively small device emanating from 238,900 miles away. Finding the answer expanded my understanding of how faith works. The signal from the moon was being received by a dish larger than the largest football stadium on earth. Likewise,

The 5 Critical Attributes Needed to Win the Faith Fight

in Matthew 9, two blind men followed Jesus asking to be healed of their blindness. When they finally cornered Him inside, Jesus asked them the greatest question of faith there is:" DO YOU BELIEVE ... I can do this?" In other words: "How great is your faith?" One Sunday morning while teaching a group of middle school children about faith, I asked the young lady if she truly believed that she was a girl. She answered "of course I do." I then asked her, "What makes you so sure?" She replied, "I am what I am and I anatomically have what I have!" Finally, I said, "What if I gave you $1 million to change your mind and become a boy?" She smiled and replied, "I'll take the money, but I'll still be a girl. No money can change that. That's who I am, that's what I am."

Recall, the story in Mark Chapter 10 about the rich young ruler who came to Jesus seeking eternal life. Jesus told him to go and give his entire riches away, take up his cross, and come follow Him. The rich young ruler went away sad and the Bible says that it was because he had great possessions. I'm not trying to correct the Bible, but I think a better interpretation of what happened would be that money had the rich young ruler.

Why is Faith Important to Please God?

Like God, we are tripartite beings. We're spirit beings, made in His image and likeness. That is to say that God is a spirit being (John 4:24), and we, likewise, are spirit beings (Thessalonians 5:23). We live in physical earth suits (bodies which allow us to connect with and work in the earth realm with five physical senses); and, we each possess a soul. The mind processes information from internal and external sources; our intellect is best defined as learning modality, understanding and operational modules that we all possess. A great military General may not be able to cook a pot of oatmeal without burning it and a 5 star chef may not be able to read a compass. They are two different intelligences. Educational researchers have identified at least seven different intelligences. They, like our various temperaments, help us to flow in our respective purpose.

Consider the lesson on prayer by Jesus: *"Our Father who is in heaven..."* We are to believe that God is real enough to talk to Him. Let's consider the pronoun "Him;" it comes from the Hebrew references for God as "Father". It literally means that God is the first head of the Trinity and the Creator/Head of all that is. God is not "the man upstairs," as He is often referred. "God is not a man," (Numbers 23:19). God is Spirit (John 4:24) and we must worship Him in Spirit and Truth. Genesis chapter 1 tells us that we are made in His image and likeness. Therefore, when we worship/relate to God in Spirit and Truth, we live our lives in constant connection with Him, just as you are in constant connection with your mental faculties (hopefully).

> *"And Elijah... said unto Ahab, As the LORD God of Israel lives, before whom I stand,"* (1 Kings 17:1)

Elijah believed God to be real and that His presence was real; more real than that which existed in his physical environment. He, in the natural, saw a famine coming; but via his connection with his Father (spiritual), he was given a plan for survival, which he followed and not only survived, but he thrived!

Faith is like a hike you've never been on. You can only trust in the words of experienced hikers who have already been down that path. Like faith, you won't see evidence that the final destination is worth it until you take the first steps.

Louis Zamperini was a person of faith, even though he lost his way, at times. When I read his amazing story and watched the movie *Unbroken*[iii]—about how he faced trauma, PTSD (Post Traumatic Stress Disorder) and alcoholism—I could relate. And, like Zamperini, faith has played an important role in my sobriety, and my life. However, Louis' life was definitely more dramatic than mine has been.

Louis became an Olympic track star and then a military officer in World War II. His plane was shot down, and he survived for forty-seven days on a life raft in the middle of the ocean. Then, he was captured by the Japanese and tortured as a prisoner of war. "To hope against all hope" means we hope for something, even though it is impossible to see how it could happen. When Louis and his comrade had been adrift in the raft for several days without water, there was no rain in sight. Yet, against all hope, he prayed and asked God for strength to endure not just for himself, but for those with him. He promised God to commit his life to Him if He'd send rain. The next morning, there was a huge downpour. The very definition of faith means to believe in that which we cannot see. Zamperini, the great American Olympian and WWII POW endured many difficult trials. In a post war interview, he quoted, "We tend to think that life would be great if we didn't have to deal with trouble and pain—if everything could just be easy. Yet, if that were the case, we wouldn't be able to learn and grow in faith. I have often wished I didn't have to go through the trials I have faced. Yet, I have to admit, I am so grateful for the strength and increased faith I have gained because of my challenges. 'No pain, no gain' applies to faith."

Only three men survived the plane crash, and only two lived forty-seven days at sea. It was Zamperini's faith and persistence that helped pull them through. However, at some point during the two years, he was a prisoner of war and frequently beaten by a guard called "the Bird;" he lost faith. He questioned how a loving God could let such things happen. After returning to the United States and getting married, he still felt like God had been "toying" with him. He began drinking heavily and got angry whenever his wife went to church. Four more years passed before Louis returned to church where he remembered the promise he had made to God before it rained. Then, he went home and emptied out all the liquor bottles in his cabinet. He never had another drink. Even though it took years, Louis still managed to find faith again and it helped him overcome.

For years after the war, Louis longed to hunt down "the Bird" to get revenge. With divine help, he finally found freedom from his prison of hatred. When he learned of the Bird's death, "something shifted sweetly inside of him." It was forgiveness, beautiful and effortless and complete. For Louis Zamperini, the war was finally over.

For me, it has been important to realize that my hatred for those who committed serious sins against me was only hurting myself. And forgiving them didn't mean they were being "let off the hook." It meant that I was being released from the strongest emotions that held me bound to them—vengeance and hatred. It takes time for us to heal and reach a place of forgiveness. When we do, we often find those dark places in our heart and mind can finally be illuminated by divine light.

Faith does not come without trust, and trusting is painful. Trust and faith work hand-in-hand to produce HOPE! Without hope, all is lost. During the writing of the final draft of this book, we here in the Houston (TX) area are experiencing extreme flooding from hurricane Harvey. The initial winds blew down trees; especially those trees with shallow root systems. In a lifestyle of faith, trust is the root system. It needs to grow deeper in our souls in order for faith to grow higher in our daily walk. Daily prayer and ingestion of the Word is like adding 'Miracle Grow' to the soil of our lives.

Noah's actions satisfied the criteria for an act of faith because all he had was God's Word. No visible evidence indicated that rain was even possible! By faith Abram (later Abraham) left the comfort of his homeland and went to a land not only foreign to him, but also hostile to his kind. Abraham also committed one of the greatest acts of faith recorded in the Bible. God instructed him to take his son Isaac to an appointed place, kill him as a sacrifice unto God, then burn the lad. This is what I find remarkable: *"And Abraham said to his young men, Abide ye here with the ass; and I and the lad will go yonder and worship (sacrifice), and come again to you."* (Genesis 5:22) What? Abraham had been instructed to kill and burn his son, but he is telling his entourage that after doing what God had instructed him to do, he and the son he was to sacrifice would be back to join them! How was this going to possible? Herein is found great faith: Abraham did not know how God was going to do it! He only believed what God said earlier; that Isaac would be the beginning of a nation of people too numerous to count.

All of the evidence presented up to this point should bring us to one inevitable conclusion, we are spirit beings – we're not accidents. Even if it were not the intentions of our parents to give birth to us at the time that they did, the fact is that they only joined to make your physical body. You were sent to planet earth as a spirit being to live a purposeful life that can only be done by walking in faith.

Pleasing God is done by living according to purpose. The cherry on top is that by doing so, you are rewarded (Hebrews 11:6)

"Lord, Help My Unbelief"

In the book of Mark (9:26), Jesus answered the call of a parent whose child was suffering from uncontrolled convulsions all of his life. The father had asked the disciples to heal the child, but their best efforts were fruitless. Jesus referred to them as "faithless". Jesus was reminding them that all things will be possible to those who believe and ask in faith. Asking the father of the child if he believed that the child's healing was possible; the father replied, "I believe, but where my faith is short, help my unbelief." We all experience times when we feel that our faith is weak. After the above mentioned incident in Mark, the disciples asked Jesus why they could not cast the demon of infirmity out of the child. Jesus told them that this type of faith action required praying *and* fasting. What's the purpose of fasting? How should we fast? Fasting is a tool that has been widely used by God's people throughout history, and it continues to be a powerful way for Christians to deepen their relationship with God. But how should you fast? Simply avoid whatever is taking your personal, intimate time with God. Or in other words, stay away from it! For example, you know that you should spend time reading your Bible and in communion with God, but you cannot resist that television. Therefore, you should try maybe twenty-one days of absolutely no television. Simply remove, deprive your flesh and your emotions, those things that interfere with receiving and connecting with God. Doesn't sound simple does it? We'll talk about it more in the section on developing your faith.

Growing in Faith

"And he did not do many miracles there because of their lack of faith." (Matthew 13:58)

Growing in faith requires bold action, even risk-taking. Moses risked his life returning to Egypt to face a man who could have ordered his immediate death. Michael Dell took a great risk when he started assembling computers in his off-campus dorm room. I notice that when I'm driving and there's a long line in one lane, but short in the other, I gravitate to the shorter. Knowing that I'm going to need to make a right turn shortly after the light changes, I take chance that an opportunity will present itself either through someone's slow driving or their kindness; I'll get over in time to make the turn.

Taking a risk always opens a potential for setbacks. What if I'm not able to get over to make the turn? Then, I must drive out of my way, U-turn, which will cost me time and a little inconvenience. However, when God leads us to take a risk, then He is there whether we perceived to have succeeded or failed. God cannot fail... if He leads you to take a risk, it may not always succeed in the way you think. The only true failure is when we fail to take the risk when God is leading us to do so. Sometimes, the fear of failure is the greater obstacle, than the risk itself. As a trained scientist, I don't accept the concept of a failed experiment. In his attempt to invent the light bulb, Edison[iv] experimented with no results over one-thousand times. He stated that he did not fail one-thousand times; the invention just required one-thousand steps.

How do I ask? Jesus explained it simply: "ASK THE FATHER IN MY NAME!" Why ask the Father in the name of Jesus, you may ask? Consider this: do you think the car dealership would finance a new car for you if you had bad credit? Of course not! But, what if Warren Buffett cosigned the loan? When God looks at us, He does not consider our righteous performance failures, but rather through the compassion and righteousness of His Son, Jesus the Christ.

Attribute #2

Believe In Your Covenant Right as God's Child

Attribute Number Two:

Believe In Your Covenant Right as God's Child

You must have faith in who you are based upon the greatness of your purpose. *"Thus said the Lord GOD unto Jerusalem; Thy birth and thy nativity of the land of Canaan; thy father was an Amorite, and thy mother was a Hittite."* (Ezekiel 16:3) The two most important events of your life are your birth and your nativity! Remember when God created you; He stated that your purpose was to have dominion over all the earth. Unfortunately, we have allowed society to dictate that this was intended for only a few select members of the Creation. In the big part of your mind, God said, *"Let them,"* not some of them, *"have dominion!"* Too often, we allow situations and/or circumstances "rob" us of our rights as children of the living God to take dominion over all earthly matters; which, in turn, leaves our assigned purpose undone. Let me take you out of your suspense. Your birth refers to your physical arrival on planet earth. By Nativity, I am referring to the moment you find out why God sent you. Understand that through the biological act of procreation, your parents put their respective chromosomes together and produced an "earth suit" for your earthly journey. Then, God placed you in that vessel. If your purpose goes unfulfilled, the body –the Church – is now deprived of the blessing we should have experienced via the fulfillment of your reason for being placed on this planet. You are not an accident! Even if your parents did not plan for or even want you, remember that their contribution was the DNA used to develop your earth suit (body). You are NOT the earth suit. The real you lives IN that earth suit.

One of the greatest mistakes being made by this generation is what I call "creature worship". More time and money is spent on the dressing (or undressing), development, and admiration of the creature we live in, than on the real man with the assignment. God is about building people who understand His purpose, His power, His process, His provision, and His promise. God's purpose for our lives is generically found in His Word. Please don't misinterpret what I am saying. The Bible clearly states that you should take care of your temple/body and dress it well. However, we must consider the care and concern that we place on the development and care of the 'real' man within; the one that looks like God.

Recall that earlier, we spoke about the woman with the issue of blood. What did she do about her situation? She believed! She did not say, "What have I got to lose?" or "It's worth a shot!" A Biblical definition of faith would be something that comes as a result of hearing and believing God's Word. In other words, faith believes in something (or having accepted as truth) something for which you have no control of and have no personal experience or physical evidence. Another example I normally like to use is the covenant of marriage. My wife and I have been married for over forty-five years. I believe through the preponderance of the evidence, supplied by forty-five plus years of cohabitation, that the commitment we made June 24, 1972, to live in a perpetual state of matrimony is the truth. I was raised in the church and a believing household, school, and community. Believing in God was always considered the 'norm'. That is what religion taught us.

Faith, however, is not based on religion, but rather a relationship. My wife and I have been through the majority of our lives believing that together, walking in a relationship with God and each other, all of our needs will be met. She could have said, "I do," and then weeks or years later, decide "I don't" anymore. That would have seriously damaged my belief in marriage. Like my relationship with God, she remained faithful to be with me in the good times and the difficult times.

A pastor friend of mine told the story of how he had gone to a conference out of town and during a lunch break, while waiting in line to order a meal, a very rude person jumped in front of him. He wanted to say something very *un-pastor-like*, but he noticed that he still had on his name badge. Regardless of how he felt, he was representing God and the ministry office of pastor. I feel the same way about the covenant of marriage. The ring I wear on my left hand is a constant reminder of my commitment to my wife and the covenant of marriage. Likewise, God asks us to wear His covenant promises in our hearts (spirit and soul) always having confidence that He is with us in the good and difficult challenges of life.

Here are five things that I learned from Dr. Ransom Mumba[v] concerning how we should view ourselves from God's perspective:

* God has not made anything that He is not proud of (this includes you). We may not be proud of things we have done (or

are still doing), but realize that misbehavior comes as a result of someone who simply misses their behavior! Behavior is determined by purpose, and when you don't behave according to purpose, we mis–behave. I recall that one day; our exterminator was sitting at the kitchen table with me, while his workers were completing their work. My little dog was busy barking constantly at something that was going on in the streets. I made the statement that I didn't know what was going on with that dumb dog and he reminded me that the dog was just doing his job (acting according to his purpose). His particular breed is known for being watchdogs. Not guard-dogs, because he's more afraid of his own shadow. But, he will awake in the middle of the night if he hears anything that sounds suspicious to him. Regardless of what you may think of yourself, you are blessed to be a blessing. It is your responsibility to walk out your blessing because ultimately, it will bless the rest of us.

* God's grace will overcome your faults if you let Him. However, you must make the decision to walk out the grace provided by the death, burial, and resurrection of His Son Jesus.

* No one is greater than you. Everyone has made mistakes, even you. Winners get up when they fall down and get going, because they have faith in God and who God made them.

*Never succumb to discouragement because of present or past situations or conditions. Know who you are. Princess Diana made many trips to the most poverty-stricken areas of the world. Armies of reporters and cameras followed her, because her current conditions did not erase the fact of who she was. Refuse to allow people, past events, or societal trends to direct your path. God has set your path and that path is designed to prosper you and give you purpose and a great future.

* Finally, don't assume that everything that goes wrong in your life is your fault. However, don't deny yourself the responsibility of owning the results of the choices you make.

Attribute #3

Take Corresponding Action or Kinetic Faith

Attribute Number Three:

Take Corresponding Action or Kinetic Faith

We must have confidence in who we are in Christ. Hebrews 4:2 refers to the fact that just as faith comes by hearing the Word of God, this 'faith' is of the theoretical category. This faith is not profitable or effectual until it is interwoven with corresponding faith in action, or as we say in physics, 'Kinetic Faith'. 'Kinetic' faith is faith in operation. It is the act of a Believer boldly going forth not by sight, but rather by faith in God's Word. Continuing with our case study, the woman with the issue of blood not only accepted as truth in her belief system that Jesus WOULD heal her, but she acted upon that which she believed. The Gospel states that according to her recollection and those of her family, she had been suffering with this illness for approximately eighteen years. She went to many of the medical professionals of that day and nothing they could do could help her. But, she had heard about a man named Jesus; how He had a reputation for speaking to someone or laying hands on them, and they being healed. She made the simple but profound choice to believe what she had heard. Maybe, she had been in the presence of Jesus during the time that He did one of these miraculous healings. Maybe, she heard a report of healing by someone she considered credible. By whatever means she had heard about the healing power of Jesus, she chose to believe that if she could get close enough to make some contact with Him, she would be healed.

The Condemnation Complex is a vile detriment to *kinetic faith*. Romans 14:22-23 asks, *"Where's your faith?"* Stand before God boldly, not condemning yourself, and allow Him to reveal His will for your life. Like Gideon, Barak, Samson, and Jephthah, you can overthrow evil kingdoms set up against you; like David and Samuel, you can establish justice and see God's promises fulfilled (Hebrews 11:32,33). I Corinthians 13 teaches us that the practice of faith requires hope. Psalms 40:4 says, *"Blessed is that man that makes the LORD his hope (trust)";* and, having the Lord as your trust and sure hope/confidence requires that you walk in love. There's a direct correlation between having God as your hope and dwelling in love. 1 John 4:16 reminds us that God is love and if we dwell in God, then we dwell in Love. For truly the greatest of all commands is to love

God and love your fellow man (Luke 10:27). Once you have made a decision to walk in love, you truly feel the presence of almighty God in your life; for God is love. It's easy to say but realistically, it is difficult to love someone that you have animosity towards. So many incredibly talented people fall short of their endeavors, because they are walking blind.

Dee W. Hock[vi] puts it this way (paraphrase mine): "A person with great experience is walking blind with meaningless knowledge, limited understanding, and impotent capacity to love, dangerous motivation, and poor character." I understand that loving the seemingly unlovable is challenging, but be reminded that faith is the substance of things hoped for and the evidence all things not seen (Hebrews 11:1). The development of faith requires that you, first of all, become members of the family of God; that is to say, you have believed and received the death, burial, and resurrection of His Son, Jesus Christ. Then, you must know that you have the power of all already working in you, at all times. But, knowing that is not enough. For example, we know that there are radio waves in the atmosphere all around us. But, you cannot take advantage of these signals without some sort of a receiver, like an FM radio. You must know that faith begins when the will of God is known. 1 Kings 17:1 tells us that we MUST live like God is alive and He will promote you.

We must stand before Him in Christ's righteousness and be ready to serve Him, for they that serve Him will renew their strength and mount up on wings like an eagle. We MUST study God's Word and be available to proclaim God's will when and where He prompts us to. The choice to live by faith gives purpose to your life. You are not an accident. Your parents made your earth suit (body), but God made you and placed you in it on this planet for a purpose.

During a challenging time as a college student, I needed a God that would answer soon, or my dream of a college degree was going to end. Recalling a 15th-year birthday card I received from my mom which said, "If you have the faith the size of a mustard seed, you can ask and it SHALL be done," I prayed, confidently, believed, and sought out to resolve my financial dilemma of needing a job. I went to an interview in the quality control department of what was then known as *Humble Oil* in downtown Houston. A position was available, but it was during my morning class time. I left that disappointment saying, "Today, God is going to find me work." Walking to the elevator, I heard the supervisor calling my name. He remembered another student in a similar situation and decided to allow us to 'split' the shift. Days later, my old evening job called me back to work and I was able to finance an entire year of classes.

The 5 Critical Attributes Needed to Win the Faith Fight

Developing a lifestyle of faith requires five elements:

- You must have the ability to see the finished work of God, regardless of the conditions/situations around you.

- Worshiping God in Spirit and in Truth develops courage and guards you against the temptations to give up. God must be the pre-eminent factor of your existence. Don't be moved by what you feel, see, or hear, but only by what you believe.

- Stewardship/Responsibility for what God has blessed you with is vital before He will trust you with more. Remember that David became the steward/King over Israel, because of his stewardship over his father's sheep.

- A sacrificial plan to give of your time, talent, and treasure is essential. Find a godly cause and commit to it!

- You have the ultimate responsibility for the overall direction of your life, not your parents, past circumstances, failures, social issues, or skin color. Can these be hindrances? Of course! But, you must go to your "War Room" and call on your Helper- the Lord God Almighty. Then, be led by the Spirit and be of good courage. Your leadership will not only affect your life, but also those who are under your care. Abandon excuses, because failure is a permitted response. YOU can do all things through Christ who strengthens you.

Kinetic faith can shut the mouths of lions seeking to destroy you and quench the fiery darts of the evil one, and win God's approval. Like David, confess that 'the Lord is your shepherd and you have no lack in Him (Psalm 23). In order to understand David's faith, remember that David was a shepherd and he truly cared for his flock. He believed that it was God's will for him to prosper, without any added sorrow. He knew that God would not force His will upon him, so he is led by still waters where sheep are not frightened or hesitant to drink.

I recall some years ago when we were in a social gathering that included our college professors. The department head shared with us somewhat of a parable. He said that, "A bird in the northern plains of the U. S. procrastinated and was late starting his journey south for the winter. Invariably, he got caught in a snowstorm that caused his wings to freeze up. Not able to fly, he landed in a field owned by a dairy rancher/farmer. The bird's plight was observed by a nearby member of the Audubon society. A 'Good Samaritan' rushed to the aide of the bird and held him in his hands, until he began to warm up. This saved the bird's life, but the man knew that he couldn't hold the bird for the duration of the winter nor long enough for him to get strength enough to continue his journey. He looked around and found some fresh, warm dung droppings left by some of the occupying cows. He chose to wrap/pack the bird in the warm feces in hopes that it would suffice until the bird could fly again. It worked! Somewhat. The bird regained his strength and felt so good about it that he began to sing. The problem came when unbeknownst to the bird, nearby was a very hungry bobcat. The bobcat approached the bird, cleaned him up, and had lunch." The moral is that it is not always your enemies that get you into it or your friends that get you out of it; but, if you are in it… please don't sing about it!

You see, in the story, there was a plan of action; thoughtful and caring, but not in the best interests of the subject. The 'prodigal son,' in a parable of Jesus', found himself in a challenging situation. When he came to himself, he searched his belief system, found a truth that he could have total faith in and not only acted on it, but rehearsed it ahead of his departure out his situation.

The story goes that a farmer's prized old donkey walked across a dry well that had only rotten boards to cover it. The animal fell into the very deep well. The farmer tried everything he could think of to get his donkey out of the well, including engaging the help of neighbors. Eventually, they all agreed that it would be in the best interest of the donkey to just shovel dirt over him and fill the well, so something like this would not happen again. But, the Donkey had a different plan of action. He had determined that his life mission wasn't over. You see, when you find yourself in a hole, there are three things that you need to do: 1) Stop digging! 2) Don't look around you for the solution; there's nothing there but dirt 3) Look up, that is where you will find a solution. As the dirt would hit his back, it hurt, but he chose to shake it off and step on it. Eventually, enough dirt was under his feet that he could step out of his once *death trap* and go on with his life.

Early in my career as an educator, I went to graduate school to obtain a master's degree in administration. Many of my colleagues and mentors thought that I would make a good administrator. At that time, I was enjoying what I was doing, teaching and coaching. But some years later, on a cold rainy night, I said to myself, "Self, this isn't fun anymore." It was at that time, that I decided to use my master's degree in administration.

First, I needed to return to graduate school and take some additional courses. One of those courses was an internship with an existing administrator. My first choice was the principal who had also been my high school principal. I was hurt when he declined my request. However, another administrator who had been a former teacher agreed to serve as my mentor. Then, I had to complete a very difficult and tedious testing battery. After failing the first attempt, God place on my "heart" a good friend and high school classmate who was currently teaching in the School of Education of a local university. He gave me some study material and I would return the next week to discuss the material, take a practice test, and awaited his return from his class. I was successful on my second attempt, but the faith fight was just beginning.

Having been taught the 'ABC's of faith, I had asked God for guidance and favor, believing in my spirit and soul that God would lead me to my destination. I now had to daily confess and thank God that I had already received what I believed Him for when I prayed. Many times every day, I thanked God for my position as a high school academic dean. Additionally, I chose to wear suits to school, instead of normal teacher attire. I was ridiculed by friends and colleagues who did not understand.

After a year of interviews, all with high ratings, I still had not been selected to the position I was believing God for. I continued to confess the manifestation of my position and God allowed me to relocate to a new classroom across the hall from the cosmetology lab. The teacher, Mrs. Suarez, saw my change in daily dress and asked why I chose to do so. When I mentioned that I was believing for a position as an administrator, she said, "So your dressing in a suit is a part of your faith confession?" Hallelujah! God had placed me close to a Believer who immediately got into faith agreement with me!

Another year passed filled with great interviews, but no promotion. Then, my greatest walk of faith came the following summer. Still a member of the coaching staff, I returned to campus early to prepare for the new season. Every week, I read the district bulletin seeking interviews with principals. There were two trainings essential for all administrators that I had not attended. I saw that they were being offered, but I had not been assigned a position, which was a prerequisite to attend those trainings. With faith in my heart, I registered for both trainings. One instructor said, "I don't know how you got into this training, because you're not on the list as a new administrator, but since you have completed the week of training, here is your certificate."

The next training required some extraordinary faith. At the beginning of preschool training for football, I asked the head coach for the week off to attend training for a position that I did not have – in the natural. To my amazement, he agreed. Prior to going to the training, I had gone to an interview at a middle school in close proximity to my school. It was with a principal with whom I have high regard. During the break of the first day of training, I called him to ascertain his selection for the position. I was not his choice, but there was obviously something he wanted to tell me that he could not. Later, he explained that during his time at the human resources office to complete the paperwork for his choice, a district superintendent who knew that he had been interviewing asked if he had any recommendations for that position in a high school that she needed to fill immediately. Without hesitation, he gave her my name. Look at God! (The rest is history.)

Attribute #4

Develop Your Faith, Don't Be a Stranger... Spend Time With God

Attribute Number Four:

Develop Your Faith, Don't Be a Stranger... Spend Time With God

Referring back to the last story told in the previous chapter, what I desired to happen in my career would never have manifested in my life if I did not believe in God's covenant promises. I had to believe that the job that I wanted was not just my "pipe dream," but moreover, it was the will of God for my life. I had to daily check the bulletin from the human resources department and speak the truth of what I believed consistently. Were there disappointments? Of course! Were there setbacks? Sure! Was there a time that I wanted to give up? Never!

People who give up and not devoted are convicted to their passion/purpose. There were three things that I needed. I cannot tell you how many times, on a daily basis, that I told myself that I would get the job. I was also encouraged by constantly thanking God for the manifestation of that job. I also encouraged myself by dressing according to an unmanifested purpose. The third thing that I needed came when I moved to a classroom that put me in an environment with another Believer. Thanks Mrs. Suarez!

Remember the story that I told you from the Bible about Abraham and the sacrifice of his own son? Before going on to the mountain to make the sacrifice of his only son, he told the men that came along with him to "stay with the asses… me and the boy will go and sacrifice and return."

Another example is when Jesus had agreed to go with Jairus to heal his daughter. Jairus must have been devastated to hear that his baby girl was dead. When Jesus arrived at the home, He found a number of non-believers crying, because they believed that hope was gone. Before He went to go see the girl, Jesus put those non-believers out of the house.

Walking in faith oftentimes requires that you leave some relationships behind you and devote yourself to living out your purpose. Your mind must be renewed day by day with the knowledge of God's Word about your circumstances. You must walk through life fearlessly and in comfort knowing that you have the rod (protection) and staff, and you're with Him (authority of God). Even in the presence of your enemies, He will anoint you with the blood of His dear Son, Jesus Christ. Mark 11:23, 24 teaches us not to doubt our God's ability or His willingness to perform His Word with signs following (Mark 16:20). <u>Believe that you always receive</u> what you ask for when you pray according to His will, which is found in His Word. Remember that faith is believing for that which you have no physical evidence. This lack of faith is described in John 20:24 when the disciple Thomas was faithless, having been told that the master had been seen. Jesus, not wanting Thomas to remain faithless, allowed him to touch areas of His flesh that proved His identity. Then, He added that those who believe without this positive, physical evidence would be happy and blessed with life abundantly. These truths must be embedded in your 'belief system' and function as an 'automatic' pilot for your life's journey.

One of the greatest leaders of the past century was Nelson Mandela. Before he transcended to go home with God, he left a great legacy of how to walk out our lives on purpose and in faith. Read these statements, from a man who was imprisoned for twenty-seven years and never lost hope or faith in the freedom of his people.[vii]

1. "Difficulties break some men, but make others. No axe is sharp enough to cut the soul of a 'Believer' (paraphrase mine)

who keeps on trying; one armed with the hope that he will rise even in the end." (From a letter to Winnie Mandela, written from the prison on Robben Island, 1 Feb. 1975)

2. "A fundamental concern for others in our individual and community lives would go a long way in making the world the better place we so passionately dreamt of." (Spoken in Kliptown, Soweto, South Africa, 12 July 2008)

3. "No one is born hating another person because of the colour of his skin, his background, or his religion. People must learn to hate, and if they can learn to hate, they can be taught to love, for love comes more naturally to the human heart than its opposite."

4. "You have to have been in an apartheid prison in South Africa to appreciate the further importance of the church. They tried to isolate us completely from the outside. Our relatives could see us only once every six months. The link was 'organizations of faithful Believers' (paraphrase mine). They were the faithful who inspired us. The WCC's support exemplified in the most concrete way the contribution that faith has made to our liberation." (Address to the 8th Assembly of the World Council of Churches, Harare, Zimbabwe, 1998)

5. "The Good News borne by our risen Messiah who chose not one race, who chose not one country, who chose not one language, who chose not one tribe, but who chose all of human

kind!" (Address to the Zionist Christian Church's Easter Conferences, 1994.)

Recall, that you are a tripartite being: Body – Soul – Spirit. Also, recall that your soul is comprised of your mind, will, imagination, emotion, and intellect. It is where decision is ultimately made. Information is received from both the external environment (the body and the world in which it resides) and the internal existential environment (the spirit man and the realm in which it resides). There are indeed three truths: 1- the good truth (one that is fabricated out of a need to justify for what one believes or wants others to believe), 2- the physical or natural truth, which reflects physical/natural laws only and 3- The spiritual and/real truth, the only truth that is true, which is the only truth that is true for all people, in all situations in all situations and for all times. Now, recall that faith believes in that for which you have no physical evidence. There is, however, spirit realm evidence if your desire is in accordance with the Word of God.

<u>Just as you feed your physical bodies worldly food, you must feed your spirit spiritual food, the inerrant Word of God.</u>

Information enters the soul via the mind synthesis, the will (desire), the intellect (study), imagination (creativity), or the emotions (feelings). This data enters the area called the conscious arena. It is sent to the subconscious where it is synthesized for an immediate response. The response may be recorded for use at a later time if the need should arise, but only if the conscience has determined the response to be truthful and appropriated. What the conscience will deem appropriate it must first be found to be truthful. Ephesians 6:14 admonishes us to gird our loins with truth.

There are two reasons why this is not talking about your physical loins (your upper thigh and pelvic region of your body). First of all, truth must be synthesized in the mind (you have no brains there). Secondly, Ephesians 6:12 has already stated that we wrestle not against flesh and blood, but against principalities, against powers, against rulers of the darkness of this world, against spiritual wickedness in high places. Since this is not a physical war, why would you need physical armor? This is spiritual warfare, so the soul must be prepared to receive spiritual truth. It is interesting that the apostle Paul used the 'loins' as an example here. It is because being a man who kept himself in good physical condition; he knew that the strongest part of the human anatomy is the loin/hip area. Likewise, the strongest arena of the soul is the mind (synthesis). Your emotions, your will, your imagination and yes, even your intellect, can be lying to you. Your mind will, under normal circumstances, accept only truth. This truth is processed via a preset of established morals, or they may have been axiomatically developed. Once the data has been received by the conscious, synthesized by the subconscious, and is accepted as truth, the information proceeds to the conscience where it can be stored and recalled, at will. This knowledge can put you on a sort of 'automatic pilot' allowing you to respond to routine input without having to process data for the best solution. If your preset of established morals has been based upon data received from the spirit man, it will reflect the perfect will of the Father. Remember, the real you, the spirit you, was made <u>by Him</u> in <u>His image</u> to do <u>His will</u>. Once the real you, your spirit man, is the main source of data supplied to your soul, then "Greater is He that is within you than he that is in the world." Also, it is His will "that you prosper and be in good health (physical and emotional), as your soul prospers and is in good health."

Attribute #5

Be Entirely Persuaded, Act Like It's Already Done!

Attribute Number Five:

Be Entirely Persuaded, Act Like It's Already Done!

"And this is the (fully persuaded) confidence that we have in Him that, if we ask any thing according to His will He hears us: And we know He hears us, whatever we ask, we know that we have the petitions that we desire of Him." (I John 5:14-15)

This brings us to the fifth of the critical attributes <u>you must be totally persuaded</u> that you were created to successfully function within the organizational structure mentioned in chapter one. Being totally persuaded means that you are in total 'Faith' agreement with God's design, how you fit into His design and function within it. You can't even truly love God without grasping this concept. Recall that God created you, because it pleased Him to do what He does best: love us! How can you love a Creator that exists as a triune 'Godhead' that you cannot physically see? This is why in Hebrews 11:6, Paul explains that the only way we can please Him (that is to say love him and most importantly, allow Him to love us) is through faith. Faith is the only tool we possess that can operate in the arena where our Creator exists and where our true being exists. Let me explain further: As I previously pointed out in Genesis chapter one, God created us in His image. John 4:24 declares that "God is a spirit..." So, since God is Spirit and He created us in His own image, then we, likewise, must be spirit beings. Another scripture that confirms this is First Thessalonians 5:23 where Paul is praying for the Believer's "spirit, soul, and body." Think on this, God did not place man, the spirit beings, into physical bodies until chapter two of Genesis (Genesis 2:7). It was then and only then that humans became what they were: "beings".

Be Totally Persuaded in your Purposeful Faith. Deuteronomy 30:18-19 instructs us to 'choose life'. This, indeed, is faith that persuades us to believe uncompromisingly. This type of belief, deeply rooted, will transcend all worldly challenges and override all acculturated solutions to those challenges. Recall, how you fell in love with your spouse. When he or she said, "I love you," you took it with 'a grain of salt'. However, the more you heard it, the more you began to believe it. Eventually, you made a conscious decision to receive it as truth. The rest of the story, good or bad, is history. If the relationship was a good one, one fact became apparent. The more opportunities that other person had to successfully demonstrate love to you; the more confident, totally persuaded, you became that the love was authentic. Even to the point that it didn't matter what anyone said about that person, he/she was "the one". I'm reminded of a love story involving two of my closest friends. Lenora and Thomas Foster started out as an unlikely couple, but have managed fifty years of marriage.

Lenora, a popular Texas Southern University student, was clerking at "Dave's Superette" at Wheeler and Scott in Houston, Texas, but she didn't want to be at work a particular Friday night. "All my friends," she kept reminding herself, "are at a party."

Thomas, the son of an East Texas Baptist preacher so strict he required assigned seating at the dinner table, popped into the store for a cold Coca-Cola. Empty bottle in hand, he'd save a nickel on the deposit in the 25-cent exchange. Or, so he thought. He hadn't counted on encountering the pretty and high spirited clerk behind the counter. "Thirty cents," she told him. "But I have a bottle," explained Thomas, who grew up in Sunnyside. She didn't see him with an empty bottle.

He didn't flinch, he didn't argue, he just paid the extra five cents. Thomas Foster had learned how to pick his battles, because he had recently been to war. "After all," thought the twenty-two-year-old soldier, "my life was already shaped by a year of combat in Vietnam and a Purple Heart." She was just a little college girl who knew nothing of the world he'd seen.

Over the following weeks, Lenora befriended a classmate who happened to be Thomas' sister. So, the store clerk and the soldier met again. On their first date, they went to the theater in downtown Houston to see *The Graduate*. Later, Lenora told her friends she'd found the man of her dreams. Also, she knew he could meet her mother's strict requirements. "Make sure he's from a Christian home," her mom used to say, "And check out his shoes. If a man takes care of his shoes, he'll take care of his wife," she said. Thomas proposed three weeks into the courtship, ultimately getting the okay from her exacting father. "He didn't cut me any slack," Thomas remembered.

On May 1, 1968, the Rev. Bill Lawson married Thomas and Lenora at Wheeler Avenue Baptist Church. After they were pronounced, Lenora started laughing and almost couldn't stop. "It was," she said, "a void filled, an overload of joy."

During the early years of their marriage, there were rough patches. They had two sons in short order, then Thomas' war experiences came back to haunt him. He had post-traumatic stress disorder long before the condition had been identified, or broad services made available. "I had it big time," said Thomas, who started self-medicating with drugs. However, Lenora was 'fully persuaded' that he was a man of God and she leaned on her faith and the Bible for direction. "I just knew my husband was a good man," Leonora said. "I knew it was going to take God for him to see who he was, so I treated him like God would have treated him. I started seeing changes after four months, but it took nine months to deliver that baby." But she was fully persuaded!

Thomas, who retired as a vice president of a local Tool company in 1998 after starting with the company as a porter, said his wife saved him from himself. In the '90s, they survived her breast cancer, and in 2008 while celebrating their 40th anniversary in Hawaii, Thomas required open-heart surgery there. The Fosters, who have two young grandsons, say they have come a long way during their decades of marriage.

Some months ago, Lenora sent me a quote that God breathed into her spirit that I found so profound that it hangs on the wall of my office. "In our early years, we struggled to make a living, but in our latter years, we shall rejoice in making a difference." It helps, they say, to be best friends. She attributes I Peter 3:1-4 as her scriptural source of strength when faith seemed hard to find.

This is the same way that you develop not only an understanding of your relationship to the triune Godhead, but an awareness of where you are to function within it. The great apostle Paul understood this principal. So he, in his letters to the Hebrews, spoke of things that they could relate to. Circumstances of the great Hebrew patriarchs who demonstrated this "God kind of Faith" that Jesus spoke of in Mark 11:22 and Hebrews 11: "by faith Abel ...by faith Enoch ...by faith Noah ...by faith Abraham ... by faith Moses ... by faith Joseph ...by faith Isaac." You may have noticed great men and women of faith in your daily lives. You've probably admired them and desired to possess their measure of faith, not realizing that you already possess your own.

One such patriarch was the prophet Nehemiah. The following story is a reprint of an article in the *Good News Magazine* entitled: <u>Nehemiah - Portrait of a Leader</u>[viii]:

The 5 Critical Attributes Needed to Win the Faith Fight

Posted on Nov 11, 1996 by Mario Seiglie:

"It may come as a surprise that the Scriptures-the Holy Bible-contain a course in leadership, given by one of the most remarkable, although little-known, leaders in the Bible: Nehemiah. His life and the principles he espoused serve as a guide to tackling life's most difficult problems. It is a classic study on successfully leading as God would have us lead: by setting an example of faith in God.

In the book of the Bible bearing his name, Nehemiah records his memoirs. He tells how, against tremendous odds, he accomplished an unimaginably difficult undertaking. Chronologically, the book of Nehemiah should come at the end of the Old Testament. Jerusalem was in ruins and surrounded by powerful enemies. Any attempt to rebuild the desolate city was met with an immediate mobilizing of forces against the Jews and was prohibited by the mighty Persian Empire, which ruled the region.

In the midst of these obstacles, Nehemiah accepted the challenge of rebuilding Jerusalem, which meant fortifying its walls, repopulating the city, and setting up for Judah a solid and God-fearing government.

The book of Nehemiah begins circa 444 B.C., some ninety years after the first group of Jews returned to Jerusalem under a leader named Zerubbabel. The temple was rebuilt, but Jerusalem as a whole, was still in ruins. A second group arrived later, led by Ezra the scribe, but the walls that should have protected the inhabitants still lay in ruin.

In those days, a city without walls could offer its inhabitants no protection and was subject to frequent raids. Few people would venture to live in such a vulnerable place. As a result, Jerusalem at that time was more of a shrine than a city. Most of the people lived outside of the gates. Against the backdrop of this desperate situation, the book of Nehemiah begins."

Survivors in Distress

Why did Nehemiah decide to go to Jerusalem? In his own words: *"Hanani one of my brethren came with men from Judah. . . And they said to me, 'The survivors who are left from the captivity in the province are there in great distress and reproach. The wall of Jerusalem is also broken down, and its gates are burned with fire.'"* (Nehemiah 1:1-3)

The 5 Critical Attributes Needed to Win the Faith Fight

Nehemiah lived in Shushan, or Susa, one of the three royal cities of the Persian Empire. The Persians had governed that part of the world for nearly a century. In chapter 2, Nehemiah tells us he was a cupbearer for the king of Persia. Nehemiah doesn't boast about his position; he just informs us what he was doing and where he was when the news of Jerusalem's disastrous plight came to him. He had many reasons to be content where he was. He lived in comfort and even splendor, and his king was pleased with him. Nevertheless, he was a Jew and deeply devoted to God. Soon, he would give up his privileged life to face enormous problems and dangers out of love for God and his countrymen.

When the news came to Nehemiah about the pitiful condition of his people in Jerusalem, he was shocked and grieved. He knew that fifteen years earlier, Ezra, the scribe, had departed with numerous Jews to rebuild Jerusalem. Nehemiah had thought the rebuilding was well on its way. Now, he heard the work had stopped and was unlikely to start up again soon. Powerful enemies were hindering the construction. A real possibility existed that Jerusalem might never be rebuilt. With hostile neighbors poised to destroy what remained of the city, including the temple, it could eventually cease from existence, altogether. Nehemiah wondered, "Would God permit Jerusalem to cease from existence?" What did he do next? *"So it was, when I heard these words, that I sat down and wept, and mourned for many days; I was fasting and praying before the God of heaven."* (Nehemiah 1:4)

In an emotional entreaty, he reminded God of His promise not to let Jerusalem perish and asked for help, so his plan to go to Jerusalem with the king's permission would succeed. His humble, heartfelt plea would be heard, and God would come to his aid. Nehemiah's prayer contains several important principles we can apply in our prayers. First, he presented himself respectfully before God. He did not begin by asking anything for himself. He came humbly before God and praised Him. Next, he confessed his negligence and imperfections and those of his people. Then, he reminded God of His mercy and favor toward those who repent and obey Him. Finally, he offered a petition that was according to the will of God. He asked for favor in the eyes of the head of state, so he could go to Jerusalem and help rebuild the walls and the government.

Months of Prayer and Preparation

Some four months later, Nehemiah writes: *"And it came to pass in the month of Nisan, in the twentieth year of King*

Artaxerxes, when wine was before him, that I took the wine and gave it to the king." (Nehemiah 2:1) The king asked Nehemiah why he looked so sad.

Although Nehemiah recognized the possibility of risk to his life, he was confident. Four months of prayer and preparation had led to this moment, and he had a few seconds to speak and find favor with his majesty. He said, *"May the king live forever! Why should my face not be sad, when the city, the place of my fathers' tombs, lies in commitment to something in the wonderment of that in the wonderment of that you have to move it over and that the amount you let me know which is surrounded and not waste, and its gates are burdened with fire?"* (Nehemiah 2:3)

Relieved to know Nehemiah's sad demeanor was not because of a plot against his life or a personal insult, the king permitted Nehemiah to speak. *"If it pleases the king, and if your servant has found favor in your sight, I ask that you send me to Judah, to the city of my fathers' tombs, that I may rebuild it."* The king asked Nehemiah how long the task would take and when he would return, then gave Nehemiah permission to go (Nehemiah 2:5-6).

Nehemiah had cleared the first hurdle with the help of prayer and diligent preparation to do God's work. Notice this principle of faith. When he petitioned the king, he had prepared beforehand all the details to help him accomplish the task. He knew he had only one chance to present the entire case before this busy ruler. He realized that, to carry out the job, he would need a travel permit, an escort of armed men, the king's written permission to rebuild, and the authority as governor to make use of wood from the royal forest near Jerusalem. He was so diligent in his preparation that he had learned even the name of the person in charge of the forest (Nehemiah 2:7-8).

So Nehemiah, out of love for God and His purpose willingly left the comfortable court life behind and as the new governor, headed with a select few toward his troubled land one-thousand miles away. More than two months later, he arrived at the devastation that was once Jerusalem and assumed duties as its governor.

Developing a Strategy

The Jews must have looked curiously at this Persian official of Jewish background who arrived with an armed escort. They probably thought he would exploit them, as had others in their long line of governors. As a diplomat and a man accustomed to court intrigues, Nehemiah said as little as possible of his plans to rebuild, since he knew enemies and spies were sure to hear him.

As part of his strategy, he *"went out by night through the Valley Gate to the Serpent Well and the Refuse Gate, and viewed the walls of Jerusalem which were broken down and its gates which were burned with fire."* (Nehemiah 2:13)

Nehemiah was disheartened to see the destruction. At that moment, Jerusalem looked to be the most insignificant and pathetic place in the Persian Empire. After Nehemiah sized up the situation, God inspired him to devise an ambitious plan to rebuild. The next day, he gathered the Jewish officials and said: *"Then you see the distress that we are in, how Jerusalem lies waste, and its gates are burned with fire. Come and let us build the wall of Jerusalem, that we may no longer be a reproach.' And I told them of the hand of my God which had been good upon me, and also of the king's words that he had spoken to me. So they said, 'Let us rise up and build.' Then they set their hands to this good work."* (Nehemiah 2:17-18)

The opposition did not sit idly by. *"But when Sanballat the Horonite, Tobiah the Ammonite official, and Gershem the Arab heard of it, they laughed us to scorn and despised us, and said, 'What is this thing that you are doing? Will you rebel against the king?' So I answered them, and said to them, 'The God of heaven Himself will prosper us; therefore we His servants will arise and build, but you have no heritage or right or memorial in Jerusalem.'"* (Nehemiah 2:19-20)

Nehemiah's bold response so shocked them that they kept a low profile for a while. Nehemiah divided up the work to be done, assigning portions of the project to various families. Nehemiah assigned the wall and the gate near the temple to the family of the high priest, Eliashib. In this way, Nehemiah gave the high priest and his kinsmen the honor of building the section with the sheep gate, which led to the temple. How proud they must have felt to build part of the wall of God's city that would become a lasting monument to their household. Chapter three of the book of Nehemiah deals with the assignments he gave to the families of the various parts of the wall. For thousands of years, their names have appeared in the Bible as a tribute to their labor.

Combating Old and New Enemies

Keep in mind that Nehemiah led by example; he also had a section to build. Imagine the governor carrying heavy beams and pieces of stonework. *"So we labored in the work . . . So neither I, my brethren, my servants, nor the men of the guard who followed me took off our clothes, except that everyone took them off for washing."* (Nehemiah 4:21-23) How encouraging it must have been for the people to see this high-ranking official lugging stones and helping defend the city!

Work began enthusiastically, but old and new adversaries, including Sanballat, began to ridicule the Jews' efforts. Before his brethren and the army of Samaria, Sanballat mockingly said, *"What are these feeble Jews doing? Will they fortify themselves? Will they offer sacrifices? Will they complete it in a day? Will they revive the stones from the heaps of rubbish-stones that are burned?"* (Nehemiah 4:2)

How did Nehemiah respond? Again, he prayed and acted on his faith. *"Hear, O our God, for we are despised; turn their reproach on their own heads, and give them as plunder to a land of captivity! . . . For they have provoked you to anger before the builders."* (Nehemiah 4:4-5)

For some time afterward, they made such progress that their enemies *"conspired together to come and attack Jerusalem and create confusion."* (Nehemiah 4:8) What did Nehemiah do? He prayed and acted. *"Nevertheless we made our prayer to our God, and because of them we set a watch against them day and night."* (Nehemiah 4:9) Nehemiah knew that praying and then hoping for a miracle wouldn't be enough.

Nehemiah gathered the leaders and inspired them to courage and faith: *"Do not be afraid of them. Remember the Lord, great and awesome, and fight for your brethren, your sons, your daughters, your wives, and your houses."* (Nehemiah 4:14) They continued building, with half the men working on the wall and half standing guard, armed with spears to keep their enemies at bay (Nehemiah 4:16).

Confronting Oppressors

You would think that now everything would go more smoothly. However, successive crises continued to befall the people. A famine had ravished the land, and many had gone in debt to feed their families. Now, they cried out when they couldn't borrow any more. Their fields and homes were being confiscated, and their children were being sold as slaves (Nehemiah 5:4-5).

The situation had become explosive. If Nehemiah mishandled the problem, the poorer people could likely revolt against the more wealthy and thus destroy their national unity and the rebuilding project. Nehemiah could have sided with the rich and influential and simply beat the people down by force of arms. But, since he truly reverenced God, he would not act this way.

Instead, here is what he did: *"And I became very angry when I heard their outcry and these words. After serious thought, I rebuked the nobles and rulers, and said to them. 'Each of you is exacting usury from his brother.' So I called a great assembly against them.'"* (Nehemiah 5:6-7) *"Then I said, 'What you are doing is not good. Should you not walk in the fear of our God because of the reproach of the nations, our enemies? I also, with my brethren and my servants, am lending them money and grain. Please, let us stop this usury!'"* (Nehemiah 5:9-10) *"So they said, 'We will restore it, and will require nothing from them; we will do as you say. . . Then the people did according to this promise."* (Nehemiah 5:12-13)

Again, Nehemiah led by his example. He was willing to freely lend to the poor, and he refused the taxes and foodstuffs that should have gone to him, as governor. He even took it upon himself to feed 150 of his countrymen (Nehemiah 5:17). In other words, Nehemiah was in effect paying a great portion of these expenses out of his own pocket. No wonder he had the respect and inspired the cooperation of his charges. Meanwhile, work continued on the wall.

Nehemiah Faces Dirty-Tricks Campaign

Since a direct attack against Jerusalem was now virtually impossible, Nehemiah's adversaries decided to try to assassinate him. They invited him to peace talks on the border between Judah and Samaria. Nehemiah adroitly excused himself from attendance and wrote them: *"I am doing a great work, so that I cannot come down. Why should the work cease while I leave it and go down to you?"* (Nehemiah 6:3)

Foiled again, the enemy now tried to incriminate him in the eyes of the Persians, imputing rebellious motives for rebuilding the walls of Jerusalem (Nehemiah 6:6-7). How did Nehemiah deal with this misinformation? Did he cringe in disbelief at the idea his king would demote him and would come to destroy Jerusalem? Did he try to work out a secret agreement with the enemy? No! He simply prayed and acted. He denied the charges and trusted God to protect him. *"Then I sent to [Sanballat] saying, 'No such things as you say are being done, but you invent them in your own heart.' For they all were trying to make us afraid, saying, 'Their hands will be weakened in the work, and it will not be done.' Now therefore, O God, strengthen my hands."* (Nehemiah 6:8-9)

Nehemiah's enemies were persistent. Since Nehemiah would not go to them, they decided to come to him. They now conspired to ruin his reputation. They apparently intended to trick him into committing a sacrilege through enticing him to enter the very temple of God. But, Nehemiah was on his toes. His intelligence agents had warned him of an informer in the Jews' midst. The double agent, Shemaiah, came to Nehemiah claiming that God had revealed to him an assassination attempt against Nehemiah and urged him to hide in the temple. Flight to the temple appeared to be a reasonable suggestion; the temple was the safest place in Jerusalem. But Nehemiah, remembering the intelligence report and realizing Shemaiah was trying to set a trap, said, *"Should such a man as I flee? And who is there such as I who would go into the temple to save his life? I will not go in!"* (Nehemiah 6:11)

By showing fear in the face of danger, Nehemiah could have disheartened those who had been inspired by his valor. By entering the temple, Nehemiah would also have been disobeying

God, because only the Levites were permitted by God's law to enter the temple. Again, Nehemiah prayed for protection from his enemies. *"My God, remember Tobiah and Sanballat, according to these their works, and the prophetess Noadiah and the rest of the prophets who would have made me afraid."* (Nehemiah 6:14)

A City Reborn from Devastation

Thanks to Nehemiah's courage, the work on the walls continued without delay. Incredibly, in less than two months, the wall was repaired. *"And it happened, when all our enemies heard of it, and all the nations around us saw these things, that they were disheartened in their own eyes; for they perceived that this work was done by our God."* (Nehemiah 6:16)

Notice, the humility and modesty of Nehemiah. He knew that God was in charge. God had enabled Nehemiah to complete this work, so he gave God all the glory. As a man of faith, he had done everything possible on his part and then had relied on God to do the rest. Finally, after nearly 150 years, Jerusalem was a city again, well-fortified and respected by surrounding nations. But, Nehemiah's problems were not over. He had to deal with additional threatening letters from his enemies. Now, however, they could do little with the city so well protected.

Spiritual Restoration and Rejuvenation

Nehemiah also turned his attention to rebuilding the spiritual foundation of the city. *"Then my God put it into my heart to gather the nobles, the rulers, and the people, that they might be registered by genealogy . . . Altogether the whole congregation was forty-two thousand three hundred and sixty . . . Some of the heads of the fathers' houses gave to the treasury of the work . . ."* (Nehemiah 7:5; Nehemiah 7:66; Nehemiah 7:71)

In this manner, Nehemiah set up the priests, gatekeepers, singers, and other people inside Jerusalem, and he reestablished the tithe, which had been neglected, to sustain the priesthood. With these people in place, the Jews celebrated the feasts of God under the spiritual guidance of Nehemiah and Ezra the scribe. Not only was the physical part of Jerusalem restored, but now came a spiritual restoration of the people, thanks largely to the example of Nehemiah and Ezra, who feared God and obeyed His laws.

Now, there was respect again for God's laws and feasts. *"So the whole congregation of those who had returned from the captivity made booths and sat under the booths [for the Feast of Tabernacles]; for since the days of Joshua the son of Nun until that day the children of Israel had not done so. And there was great gladness."* (Nehemiah 8:17)

As the Jews grew spiritually in God's sight by keeping His Feasts, they also grew in understanding of God's will. They saw more clearly their sins and neglect. They solemnly vowed to once again keep the Sabbath holy and not indulge in marriages with their pagan neighbors. They resolved to tithe faithfully. They even signed an agreement *"to walk in God's Law . . . and to observe and do all the commandments of the Lord our Lord, and His ordinances and His statutes."* They further promised to structure their society on the foundation of God's laws (Nehemiah 10:28-39).

A Leader Who Set the Standard

Who was the first person to sign this pact before God? It was Nehemiah. He knew he should set the example and not be the last one in line (Nehemiah 10:1). This was such an important pact in the history of God's people that it inspired a lasting spiritual revolution. From that time, many of God's people would faithfully keep the Sabbath and the feasts, tithe and refrain from mingling with pagan nations. That is why, nearly four-hundred years later, when Christ set up His Church, there existed Jews who were still keeping God's laws-even though the Jews had backslid many times in those four centuries.

The physical work of rebuilding the walls and restructuring their society was complete, but then came another formidable task: repopulating the city. Nehemiah first named competent administrators to serve the city, then by lot, chose some to move back into Jerusalem. One out of every ten households gave up its comfortable home outside the city and came to live in Jerusalem. *"And the people blessed all the men who willingly offered themselves to dwell at Jerusalem."* (Nehemiah 11:2)

As the city was again filled with multitudes and additional building projects were well on their way, Nehemiah realized it was time for him to leave. Now, he could go back to the king's side as his trusted cupbearer. Yet, as a good example and man of faith, he did not forget his people. He kept in touch.

The Mice Will Play

As soon as he had left Jerusalem, however, a power struggle took place. As he learned later, the high priest, Eliashib, allowed one of Nehemiah's worst enemies and an ally of the Samaritans, Tobiah, to take up a privileged office in the temple precincts. Soon, God's people were again neglecting His laws (Nehemiah 13:4).

With this influence, the Jews began socializing again with the Samaritans. They quit tithing; they ignored the Sabbath. So, Nehemiah made the difficult and frustrating journey back to Jerusalem. *"Then after certain days I obtained leave from the king, and I came to Jerusalem and discovered the evil that Eliashib had done for Tobiah, in preparing a room for him in the courts of the house of God. And it grieved me bitterly; therefore I threw all the household goods of Tobiah out of the room."* *"Then I commanded them to cleanse the rooms; and I brought back into them the articles of the house of God, with the grain offering and the frankincense. I also realized that the portions for the Levites had not been given them; for each of the Levites and the singers who did the work had gone back to his field. So I contended with the rulers, and said, 'Why is the house of God forsaken?' Then all Judah brought the tithe of the grain and the new wine and the oil to the storehouse."* (Nehemiah 13:6-12)

Why did Nehemiah so fervently and diligently serve God? Did he plan his actions so he could be seen of men? No. As Nehemiah explained in his prayer: *"Remember me, O my God, concerning this, and do not wipe out my good deeds that I have done for the house of my God, and for its services!"* (Nehemiah 13:14)

When Nehemiah returned to Jerusalem, he saw the people working on the Sabbath. *"In those days I saw people in Judah treading wine presses on the Sabbath, and bringing in sheaves, and loading donkeys with wine, grapes, figs, and all kinds of burdens . . . And I warned them about the day on which they were selling provisions."* (Nehemiah 13:15)

Again, he prayed and acted. He assigned guards to the wall to ensure that no one would work or do business on the Sabbath. He prayed, *"Remember me, O my God, concerning this also, and spare me according to the greatness of your mercy!"* (Nehemiah 13:22) Nehemiah well understood the principle, later expressed by James, that faith without accompanying works is useless: *"Do you see that faith was working together with his works, and by works faith was made perfect? ... You see then that a man is justified by corresponding actions (works), and not by faith only."* (James 2:22-24)

Solving One Final Problem

Nehemiah ends his incredible account by tackling one last problem, that of marriages between Jews and pagans, of the people of God socializing and marrying into families that worshiped false gods. His zeal, as a right example of obedience to God, never faltered. *"So I contended with them... saying, 'You shall not give your daughters as wives to their sons, nor take their daughters for your sons or yourselves... Thus I cleansed them of everything pagan...'"* (Nehemiah 13:25; Nehemiah 13:30)

After a bountiful life filled with faith, Nehemiah ends his remarkable life story by asking God to do what all of us would surely ask for: *"Remember me, O my God, for (my) good (faith)."* Nehemiah was fully persuaded that God had a plan to restore the homeland of his people. He was also fully persuaded that he was the person through whom God would manifest this great work. He looked beyond the situation, his background, and his age.

The 5 Critical Attributes Needed to Win the Faith Fight

The Bible records a story told by Jesus about the master of the house who left different degrees of talent with his servants. Upon returning, they had multiplied the talents given for good. All except one. This person, of little or no faith, gave all kinds of excuses as to why he had not done according to the dictates of his purpose.

Conclusion:
The Covenant of Faith

Why believe? You can't be fully persuaded by joining a body of believers, because of family tradition. As a child, I did. I was convinced that God was real, but if I was asked why I believed, I couldn't answer. My total confidence came through my travel experiences. I'm blessed to be married to a travel agent and have the opportunity to see many parts of the world. I have seen evidence of early civilizations with their altars/temples of sacrifice to their 'gods'. Even with no true knowledge of the one true God, they knew that there were undeniable benefits by the shedding of blood. The early Jews sacrificed animals. The head of the household would place his hands on the head of the lamb symbolizing the transfer of the sins of the family to that innocent animal. Jesus, the Son of God, brought the ultimate message: *"Enough! My blood, once and for all!"*

While attending class in the Ransom Mumba School of Ministry[ix], a fascinating discussion on covenant leaped its way onto the final pages of this book (with permission).

Covenant is one of the Scriptures most prominent themes, and yet it is little discussed in the church in the 21st century. While many might be able to name the famous covenants or point to one here or there, too many Christians struggle to explain them in detail and highlight their significance for us today. Covenant is high on God's agenda, because it is the heart of who He is. A relational God chose to, and continues to, relate with us on the basis of His covenant with us. Without understanding the covenant of faith, our relationship with God, although sincere and heartfelt, will be without the most significant attribute that we may possess to please him – faith. For this is the essence of who God is and how He operates in faith with us.

Covenants are not only between man and God. We make covenants with our fellow man often on a daily basis. The Bible talks about the covenant between men. For example, Laban and Jacob, Jonathan and David, and Abraham and Abimelech all had various covenants made between them. In addition to these scriptural references, a covenant is a well understood concept in life at many levels. A covenant can be made between two nations or people groups that would allow trade, inter – marriage, or to coexist in peace. We often see the act of covenant in many marriage ceremonies today. A member of the bride's family would light a family candle and likewise, the groom's family would also light a candle. The ceremony would end with the groom retrieving the candle representing his family and the bride doing the same. They would then light a single candle on the altar representing a covenant that has now been made between the two families, as a result of the marriage covenant.

The English word 'covenant' derived from two Latin words: *venire* and *con* which means come together. In Hebrew, the word for covenant (found primarily in the Old Testament) is *'Berit'* and *'Diatheke'* (Greek) is found primarily throughout the New Testament. Many biblical scholars believe that the word *BERIT* derived from the noun – *Barah* which means to eat. It was in biblical days, and still today, a way of celebrating a new covenant. For example, the meal after the wedding ceremony celebrates a new covenant. A covenant is more than an agreement. A covenant represents a completed bond without hidden agendas and once established it cannot be broken.

The relationship between God and man is based on *faith*. God relates to us on the basis of His covenant and in doing so, He is affirming His commitment, presence, and intention towards His people. In the book of Jeremiah, God said, *"I will be your God and you will be my people."* In Genesis chapter 17, God states that His covenant with us is everlasting. God's covenant relationship tailor-made to our understanding. Abraham was a Chaldean of Ur. When the Chaldeans established a covenant between one another, they would split open a sizable animal then joined their hands and together walk through the two pieces of flesh, signifying that should one of them break the covenant they had made; their blood would spill on the ground like the animals they walked between. Abraham did not walk between the pieces of flesh. God had to walk through the covenant pieces with Himself to signify that He would not break His covenant with the children of Abraham. All of God's covenants (with the exception of the Mosaic covenant) are not about rules, but about relationship!

The people of the early church understood that covenant was somewhat like a contract in that the parties involved would come together, agree, and accept the obligations and the terms that were to be carried out by each one, and then live within the framework of that agreement. In essence, this was seen as an agreement between equals! Of course, we know that God is not a man. But, we must be reminded that when God created the birds, He spoke to the air; when He created vegetation, He spoke to the earth; when He created sea creatures, He spoke to the water; but, when He created man, He spoke to Himself! The Bible says that He created us to be just a little lower than the angels. That means that literally, we are in His inner circle of equality. The Bible states that God is full of love, grace, mercy, and compassion and we have access to all of it via the covenant sacrifice of His Son, our Savior and elder brother – Jesus.

While in the class, I was asked to express what covenant meant to me? Simply put, I can only say that my covenant with God means that I do not have to live in the mistakes of my past, but rather rejoice in the wonderment of my future!

What are you doing with the life you have been given? Will the trail that you are blazing on the earth make life better for those who follow? "Keep the Mustard seed, baby!"

About the Author

Dr. Paul Denman is the founder and executive director of Ephraim Foundation, a collaboration of Christian counselors whose purpose is to equip the body of Christ with tools of relationship enhancement and/or augmentation. He is a Licensed Belief Therapist board certified by the Therapon Institute. Under the guidance of the Holy Spirit, he specializes in relationship reconciliation and restoration of marriages and families.

Dr. Denman along with his wife, Henrinetta, also a board certified Belief Therapist, counsel through their practice, Compassion Christian Counseling. In addition to his counseling ministry, Dr. Denman trains Christian counselors through the Therapon Institute and provides continuing education training for health care providers in the Houston area. Outreach ministries established from their practice include: REAL Marriage - Houston, Man Alive Men's Fellowship, and The Ephraim Project. Dr. Denman serves on the board of directors for Youth Exchange Services and R.E.A.P. center for veterans.

Other endeavors include: El Shaddai International Christian Center, former member of the New Light Christian Church as a youth minister where he graduated from the Ministry Development Institute. He serves on the talent search and scholarship committees of his Fraternity, Omega Psi Phi, Inc. He believes his two greatest accomplishments is being a child of God and married to the same woman for over forty-five years.

Bibliography

---

[i] *Understanding Your Potential*. Monroe, Myles. Copyright 1991 / Revised 2002. Destiny Image Publishers, Shippensburg, PA USA.

[ii] *Looking Forward Magazine*. Anderson, H. Winston. Copyright 2010. iUniverse Publishing Bloomington, IN.

[iii] *Unbroken: A World War II Story of Survival, Resilience and Redemption*. Hillenbrand, Laura. Random House Publishers Copyright, 2014. New York, NY.

[iv] *The Edison Papers*. Rutgers, The State University of New Jersey. Piscataway, NJ.

[v] *Understanding Your Covenant Rights*: Sermon by Dr. Ransom Mumba, Pastor: Relentless Church, Spring, TX.

[vi] *Birth of the Chaordic Age*. Hock, Dee W. Barrett-Koehler Publishers 1st Edition January, 2000.

[vii] *Long Walk To Freedom: The Autobiography of Nelson Mandela*. Little, Brown and Co. 1st Edition, 2008.

[viii] *Profiles of Faith: Nehemiah - Portrait of a Leader*. Seiglie, Mario. Good News Magazine: November - December 1996.

[ix] *Understanding God's Covenants*: Mark Pease, Lecture Sunday, September 16, 2017. Ransom Mumba School of Ministry, Relentless Church, Spring, TX.

www.ingramcontent.com/pod-product-compliance
Lightning Source LLC
Chambersburg PA
CBHW070854050426
42453CB00012B/2201